First Facts®

Your
Body
Systems

Your Muscular System Works!

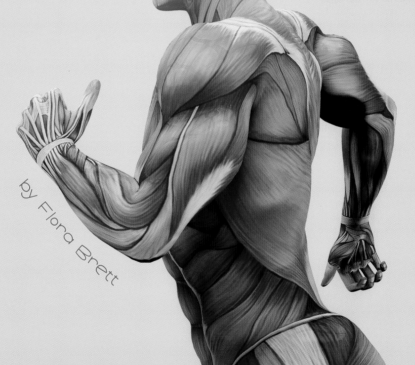

by Flora Brett

CAPSTONE PRESS
a capstone imprint

First Facts are published by Capstone Press,
1710 Roe Crest Drive, North Mankato, Minnesota 56003
www.capstonepub.com

Library of Congress Cataloging-in-Publication Data
Brett, Flora, author.
Your muscular system works! / by Flora Brett.
    pages cm. — (First facts. Your body systems)
Summary: "Engaging text and imformative images help readers learn about their muscular system"—
Provided by publisher.
Audience: Ages 6–9.
Audience: K to grade 3.
Includes bibliographical references and index.
ISBN 978-1-4914-2065-2 (library binding) — ISBN 978-1-4914-2249-6 (pbk.) —
ISBN 978-1-4914-2271-7 (ebook PDF)
1. Musculoskeletal system—Juvenile literature. 2. Muscles—Juvenile literature. 3. Human physiology—
Juvenile literature. I. Title.
QP301.B83 2015
612.7—dc23
                                2014023831

Editorial Credits

Emily Raij and Nikki Bruno Clapper, editors; Cynthia Akiyoshi, designer;
Svetlana Zhurkin, media researcher; Laura Manthe, production specialist

Photo Credits

iStockphotos: Christopher Futcher, 19; Shutterstock: Alila Medical Media, 15, AntiMartina (dotted
background), cover and throughout, ClipArea Custom media, 11, DM7, cover, 1, Jacek Chabraszewski, 20,
martan, 5, michaeljung, cover (top right), back cover, 1 (top right), Oleg Mikhaylov, 17, Sebastian Kaulitzki, 13,
Sergieiev, 21, Valentyna Chukhlyebova, 9, Viacheslav Nikolaenko, 7

Printed in the United States of America in North Mankato, Minnesota.
092014   008482CGS15

Table of Contents

Marvelous, Moving Muscles

Without **muscles**, you couldn't walk, talk, eat, or even breathe! More than 630 muscles make up your muscular system. They help you move, lift, and push.

Muscles come in four shapes. The biceps and triceps in your arms are spindle shaped. Your forehead muscle is flat. The deltoid in your shoulder is triangular. The muscles around your mouth and the pupils of your eyes are circular.

muscle—a tissue in the body that is made of strong fibers

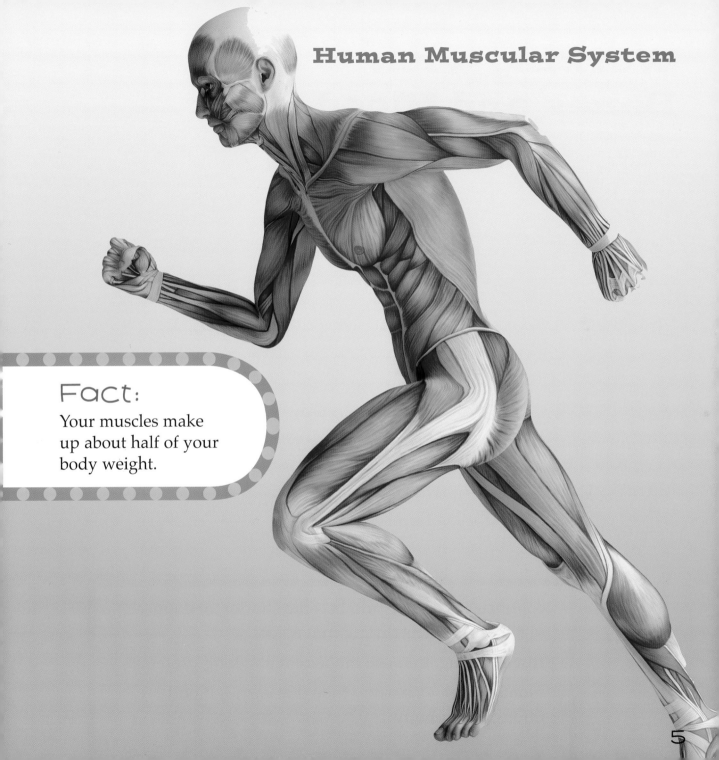

Fact:

Your muscles make up about half of your body weight.

Working with Bones and Blood

When you run or throw a ball, your muscles **contract**. Tiny threads of protein in your muscle **fibers** get closer together. Some muscles are attached to bones. The bones move when contracted muscles pull on them.

Muscles along your **blood vessels** control what body parts get the most blood. When you run, more blood goes to your legs. When you eat, more blood goes to your stomach.

contract—to tighten and become shorter; one muscle in a pair contracts during movement

fiber—a long, thin cell made of many long proteins

blood vessel—a narrow tube that carries blood through your body

Fact:
Muscles pull but cannot push.

Parts of the Muscular System

Muscles can be big, like in the legs. Or they can be small, like in the face. Your face has more than 30 muscles. They help you show different feelings. Eye muscles are the busiest.

Tendons and **ligaments** complete the muscular system. Tendons attach muscles to bones. Ligaments connect bones to bones. Muscles crisscross the body so you can move in many ways.

tendon—a strong, thick cord of tissue that joins a muscle to a bone

ligament—a band of tissue that connects bones to bones

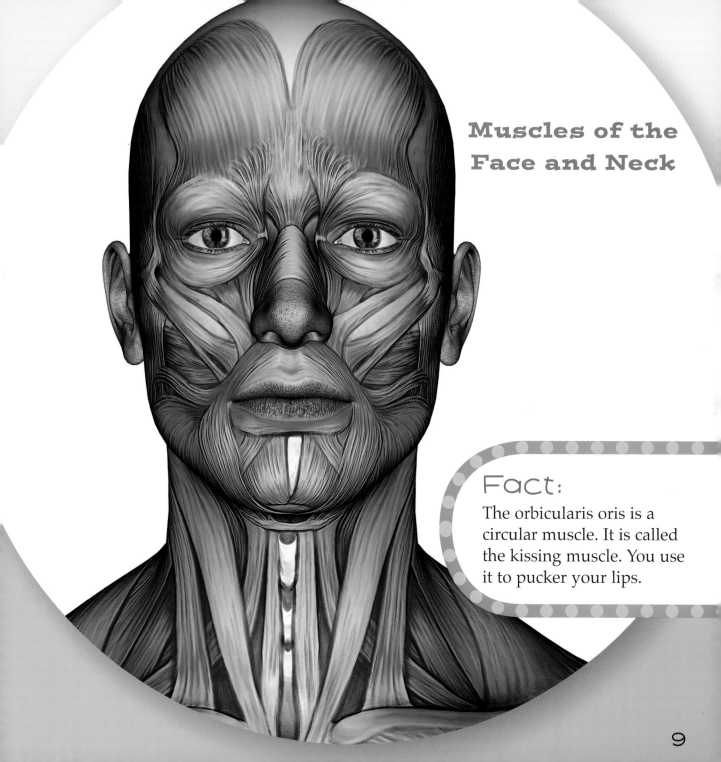

Muscles of the Face and Neck

Fact:

The orbicularis oris is a circular muscle. It is called the kissing muscle. You use it to pucker your lips.

Skeletal Muscles

Skeletal muscles move bones. These muscles are **voluntary** muscles. You control them and move them on purpose. The strongest skeletal muscles are connected to the spine.

The **biceps** and **triceps** are skeletal muscles. They move in pairs to pull in different directions. Imagine that you are throwing a ball. Your biceps pulls your lower arm up. Your triceps pulls it back down.

voluntary—controlled and done on purpose

biceps—the muscle on the front of a person's arm responsible for bending the arm at the elbow

triceps—the muscle along the back of the upper arm

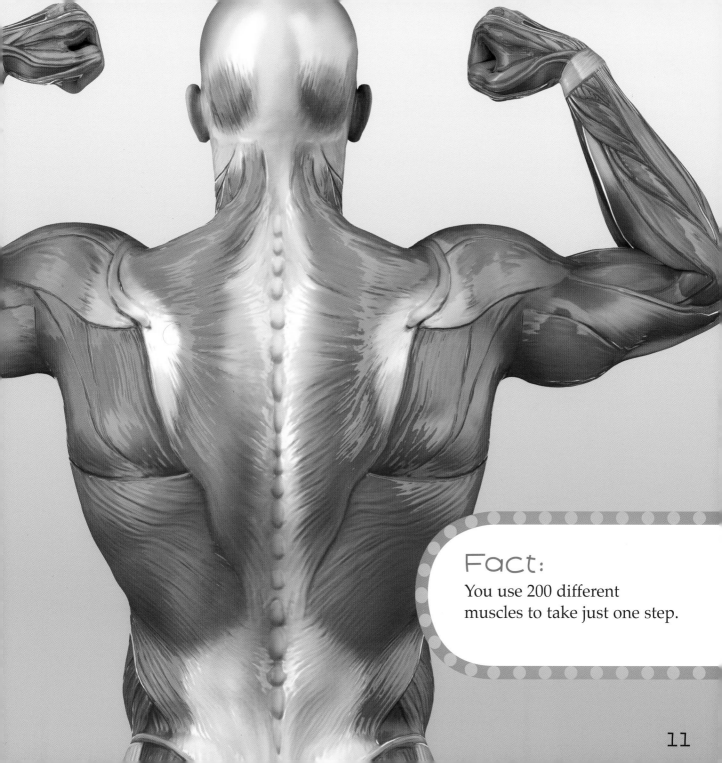

Fact:
You use 200 different muscles to take just one step.

Smooth and Cardiac Muscles

Smooth muscles and **cardiac** muscles are **involuntary** muscles. You don't think about making these muscles move.

Your organs have smooth muscles. Some smooth muscles help blood flow. Others help food move. Bladder muscles contract to hold urine in. Then they relax to let urine out.

Your heart's cardiac muscles pump blood. These muscles work with your lungs to put **oxygen** into your blood.

cardiac—having to do with the heart

involuntary—done without a person's control

oxygen—a colorless gas that people and animals breathe

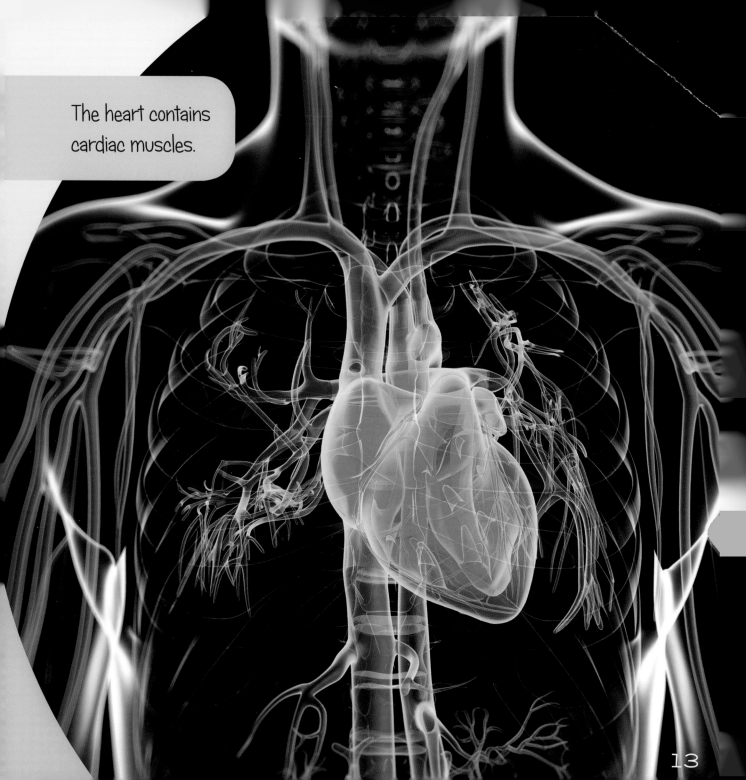

The heart contains cardiac muscles.

Muscles and Nerves

Your brain uses nerves to send messages to your muscles. Nerves are thin fibers that send messages between your brain and other body parts. Imagine you are drawing a picture. Your brain tells your hand muscles to move.

Other nerves signal your cardiac muscles to squeeze automatically. Each time your heart squeezes, it makes a heartbeat.

Fact:
A six-year-old's heart usually beats between 60 and 95 times per minute.

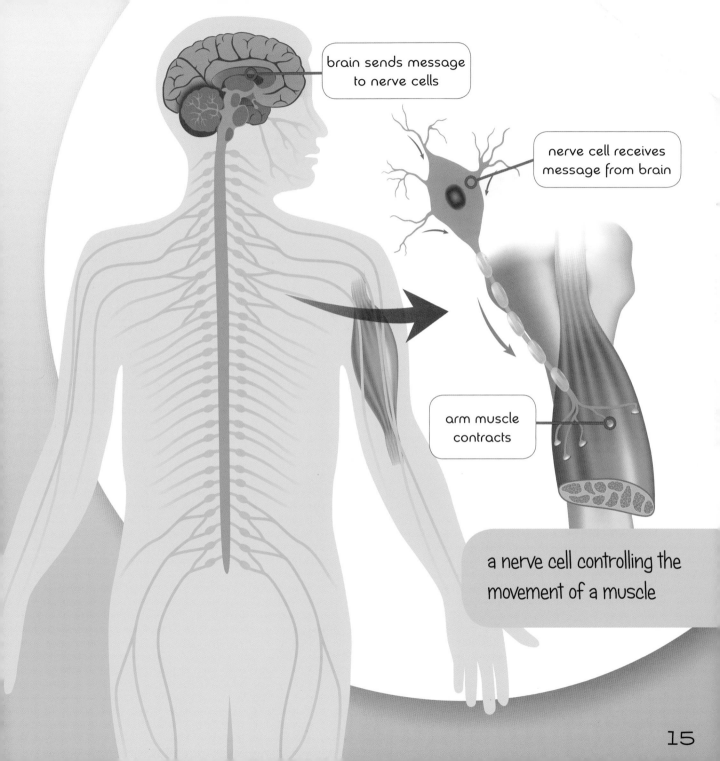

brain sends message to nerve cells

nerve cell receives message from brain

arm muscle contracts

a nerve cell controlling the movement of a muscle

Muscular System Problems

Muscles sometimes hurt. Too much exercise can make muscles sore or cause a cramp. A cramp, or **spasm**, happens when a muscle contracts but doesn't relax again.

A pulled muscle has been stretched too far. It usually feels better within a couple weeks. A **sprain** is a pulled or torn ligament. This is a more serious injury. It takes longer to recover.

Fact:
The ankle is the most common area for a sprain.

spasm—a sudden tightening of a muscle that cannot be controlled

sprain—an injury caused by muscle and tissue tearing near a joint

17

Keeping Muscles Healthy

Healthy muscles are strong and **flexible**. Exercise makes muscles stronger. Stretching makes muscles more flexible. Regular exercise helps your muscles work better. Your heart gets better at pumping.

Warm up your muscles before you exercise. This protects you from injuries. When you warm up, your heart beats faster. More blood flows to your moving muscles.

flexible—able to bend

19

Team Players

Your muscles are always working! The muscular system works with other body systems. It keeps you healthy and active. Muscles, bones, and nerves help you move, feel, and get strong. When you eat right and exercise, your body works at its best.

Amazing but True!

Have you ever gotten goose bumps? Tiny muscles surround each hair in your skin. When you're cold or scared, those muscles contract involuntarily. This causes the hairs to raise. Your skin looks like it has little bumps.

goose bumps

Glossary

biceps (BY-seps)—the muscle on the front of a person's arm responsible for bending the arm at the elbow

blood vessel (BLUHD VEH-suhl)—a narrow tube that carries blood through your body

cardiac (KAR-dee-ak)—having to do with the heart

contract (kuhn-TRAKT)—to tighten and become shorter; one muscle in a pair contracts during movement

fiber (FYE-bur)—a long, thin cell made of many long proteins

flexible (FLEK-suh-buhl)—able to bend

involuntary (in-VOL-uhn-ter-ee)—done without a person's control

ligament (LIG-uh-muhnt)—a band of tissue that connects bones to bones

muscle (MUHS-uhl)—a tissue in the body that is made of strong fibers

oxygen (OK-suh-juhn)—a colorless gas that people and animals breathe

spasm (SPAZ-uhm)—a sudden tightening of a muscle that cannot be controlled

sprain (SPRAYN)—a pulled or torn ligament

tendon (TEN-duhn)—a strong, thick cord of tissue that joins a muscle to a bone

triceps (TRY-seps)—the muscle along the back of the upper arm

voluntary (VOL-uhn-ter-ee)—controlled and done on purpose

Read More

Korb, Rena B. *My Muscles*. My Body. Edina, Minn.: Magic Wagon, 2011.

Parker, Steve. *How Do My Muscles Get Strong*? Inside My Body. Chicago: Raintree, 2011.

Wheeler-Toppen, Jodi. *Human Muscles*. Fact Finders: Anatomy Class. Mankato, Minn.: Capstone Press, 2010.

Internet Sites

FactHound offers a safe, fun way to find Internet sites related to this book. All of the sites on FactHound have been researched by our staff.

Here's all you do:
Visit *www.facthound.com*
Type in this code: 9781491420652

 Check out projects, games and lots more at
www.capstonekids.com

Critical Thinking Using the Common Core

1. What are the three muscle types? What jobs do they do? (Key Ideas and Details)

2. Can you remember a time when your muscles felt sore? Why do you think your muscles got sore? How could you keep your muscles from getting sore again? (Integration of Knowledge and Ideas)

3. Why do you think it's important to keep your muscles and body healthy? (Key Ideas and Details)

Index